Metamorphosis

Written and Illustrated By: Aly Mackenzie MacDonald

Dedication

To the lovers, the fighters, the breakers, the menders
To the curious, the all-knowing, the simple, the complex
To the tired, the weak, the lonely, the self-isolated
To the healed, the optimistic, the hopeful, the empowered

© 2023 AlyMac Publishing

All rights reserved. This book may not be reproduced
in part or in whole in any form.

ISBN: 979-8-218-97319-3

Acknowledgments

This year (2023) I embarked on an unexpected journey, and was met with open arms, able minds, and industrious hands. These poems started out as a coping mechanism but became so much more.

To the creatives,

Thank you, to every person who helped me make this a reality. I could not have done this without your help and constant support. So many hands went into creating this book you hold today. This would merely have been a dream, were it not for the wonderful people who came alongside me. I would like to thank my family for always encouraging me to create and make a difference. I would also like to give special thanks to Gina Presson and Carol Brinson for editing this work, to Stacey Panson for formatting this manuscript, and to Breana Ross for her guidance in the publication process. I cannot believe that after months of hard work, **Metamorphosis** *has come to fruition.*

So, from the bottom of my heart,

Thank you.

Introduction

Some may argue that actions speak louder than words, while others may argue that words speak volumes.

As you read, I hope the decibels will amplify with each turn of the page.

As you read, I hope you will see how I compare our growth to that of a butterfly.

> **To Create** – a small egg that lands on a bright green leaf, that will become food for the hatchling.
>
> **To Discover** – the growing larva learning about the earth it now inhabits.
>
> **To Fester** – feeling trapped in a suffocating cocoon, knowing it will not stay there forever.
>
> **To Soar** – finally spreading it's colorful wings and taking flight.

I value words: the stories they tell, the weight they hold, and the impact they have. I do not wish for this to be a typical read, but one that causes you to think, perhaps reflect, but more importantly, to feel.

In your hands you hold the purest form of my heart, or as close to it as you may get. I challenge you to listen to my pulse change pace with the intensity of the poems, to listen to me breathe with the pages as you run your finger along the edge of the paper to turn it over, and to feel my heart flutter as you flip through the pages to find your place.

I officially turn my heart over to you, handle it as you wish.

Table of Contents

To Create 6-16

To Discover 17-35

To Fester 36-56

To Soar 57-82

To Create

Breaking Water

The faucet leaks fluid crystal clear
The rhythmic sound of dripping all I hear
As my limp body takes float I feel fear
Adding to the rising water my singular red tear

No safety in sight, stranded, no lifeboat,
Left to my resources I hold my breath to bloat
To hopefully keep my limp body afloat
Thinking a crocodile in a vast freshwater moat

Now a sea of black and white my head remains
Lungs collapsing, I embrace the pains
My limp body sinking, ankles tied to vital chains
Eyes closed, blood coursing through my veins

The drain plug is pulled as the water retreats
Lying in darkness, my heart irregularly beats
My limp body bathed in heat clothed in white sheets
A deep breath in, a bright light my eye greets

This Chapter is Called: Beauty

The beginning was beautiful
Too beautiful to tell
Like something from a movie or a storybook
But if I do tell you may not believe me
So this chapter I will keep to myself

Auction

You say you saw me from across the room
And as I cautiously walked by you caught a whiff of my perfume
And you were sold

In Bloom

A flower in a field of ice
Its bright petals seem to entice the bees that buzz by
Landing and pollinating promptly
The fruitful plant leaves behind seeds
That the birds pick up as they breeze by
Carelessly dropping the seeds on their flight home
Enabling more growth that covers the earth
As vibrant flowers take birth

Heart on the Sleeve of My Book

I lead a simple life with simple needs
And I wear my heart on a shelf

Stacked high for the world to see
My emotions and the deepest inner parts of me

Always stocked to the brim with books
And books on how to read me

Dancing in the Rain

My mother always told me not to dance in the rain
Because a draft or a cold I would obtain

But as we ran to hide from the tears of the sky
You presented your hand and waited for a reply

I placed my hand in yours and I looked you in the eyes
And we danced round under the moon's cries

Passing Through

I do not want to be another picture in your hallway

Because people in hallways are only ever passing through

A Small Scream

I spin and I spin and I lose my spot
Till my head gets dizzy but my finger I focus
On like a dot
Hidden in a painting of swirls

The Silence of Your Presence

I used to avoid eye contact like the plague
Hide the pure joy I felt when you were near
And hush my happy thoughts that I wanted to
Pour onto you like a tidal wave
Crashing against a lonely beach

Because somehow even in your beautiful presence
I felt alone

Head Over Heels

I fell so hard for you
So hard that I landed flat on my face
And broke my nose
Am I good enough for you yet?

To Discover

Showers and May Flowers

It's foggy outside today
Think an opaque shade between pale blue and gray
It's pretty and mysterious and full of wonder
But soon interrupted by a booming thunder

The rain comes down
Tearing through the fog like little needles aiming for the ground
Sharp and accurate precisely nailing the bullseye
When all the fog has dissipated the rain lets out a sigh

It was foggy outside today
But the rain swept through like the spring does in May
Bringing showers and flowers and long day hours
Perfectly mimicking the nursery rhyme that was once ours

But the rain came down
And flooded the earth and the beautiful flowers now drown
We must have missed that part of the verse
Or maybe it was forgotten to spare us from the curse

Seasons

Blossom and bloom, rain and sun.
Dandelions and flowers, frolic and run.
Down the grassy hills of bright green,
Vibrant and indicative of life, serene.

Rain and sun, humid and hot.
Sailing the ocean in a pearly white yacht.
Foe or not, one goal remains,
Enjoy what is left of the quickly dying plains.

Orange and yellow, and rustling wind.
Leaves fall as if, the trees have been skinned.
Cool air travels around the earth,
As an icy trail blazes, and winter takes birth.

Rustling wind, frost and snow
Flowers and trees are perishing slow.
Everything inevitability lurches to a halt,
Forever frozen in a lock and key vault.

Poor Planter

You allowed my heart to blossom
And because your knowledge of plants was limited
You took shears to my beautiful flowers

Time

Why is time never on our side?
An invisible barrier like the rise of the tide
A force that repels us further
And further until I hear not a murmur.

No sign of life, no pulsing heart,
Left with broken pieces yet I must restart.
But there is an ear-splitting tick-tock
A constant reminder of our inevitable block.

Why is time never on our side?
Not bound to emotions, nothing to hide.
Like clockwork, you will pass me as I you
But how can I miss what I never fully knew?

Take Cover

You did not have to come and blow up my life
I lived this long without you
I was fine
And when you realized
You ran for cover and watched me implode

Before and After

I suffered before you
And I suffered after you

But I wish there was no after you
I wish I was content with life before you

The Red Thread of Fate

A myth I let my twisted mind believe
When you told me that you would never leave
And so I built a life for us
A house and a car and a dog named Gus

Tied around our fingers a bright red string
Good enough for now until a real ring
A strong line that can never be severed
Or so says the myth as it thinks us tethered

But when I moved left you would not follow
And soon enough your chest felt hollow
I'd lie my head down to hear your heart
Phantom beat after beat unevenly set apart

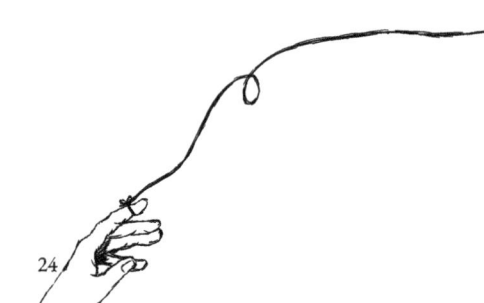

While I was away our string was not taut
Not beckoning me back home like I thought
Yet you were so far so why no strain?
My heart felt heavy stricken with pain

I came back home but only to find
Your string went through me was I dumb? Was I blind?
As you fell asleep I followed the red glow
Out of the house down the street and what do you know?

Tied to someone named Sleeping Beauty
Her body encased in red string heavy-duty
I trudge back home in the pouring rain
I pack my things and leave not a crumb for your brain

You do not deserve to know how I feel
How I now have to decipher what is false from real
And if my bright red string is not tied to you
Then I will untie my string if it is the last thing I do

Moving Trains

I wish love was like a moving train
Once you're on
There is no getting off

But there is always an out
You can pull the string that sends a
Ding to the conductor to halt the locomotive
Or you could do the unthinkable

But in a perfect world
Where no one gets off a
Moving train

That
That is what
I wish love was like

Tainted Tea

The kettle hisses
I push out my chair and walk over to the stove
You pour the hot water into my tea cup
I sit down

I steep the tea bag
- Hold the milk -
Add one lump of sugar
Maybe two

Stir and sip
I fall out of my chair I wipe my lips
My hand is stained purple
Above me a shadow of a man I once knew

You step into the light
Holding the stem of Wolfsbane

Reflections Reveal

Fighting fragile feelings, and finally facing my fear.
Chrystal clear concept,
Yet cloudy clouds cloud my judgement.

Afraid and apprehensive of ultimately being alone.
Everybody expresses that everyone has someone,
Ever emphasizing my emphatic attempt.

Nervous now, for new names abound.
No thoughts, trying merely to test my fate,
Trial and error, yet terrible tries tend to come up dry.

Unaware of the damage done; doubting the impact.
Backing into a mirror, baffled by wounds I bare.
Black and blue, battered and bruised.

This is why I want to win but
Gold is going, going, gone.
I've got grit but I'm garnished with naive good.

I'm unwanted, used, useless even.
I want what others have, hating my now hardened heart.
But I'm healing, housing my heart, for others will not.

Talking to Myself

Often I sit and talk to myself
Talk to the walls or the books on the shelf

It was no different when you were around
Because nothing to you was important unless your name would abound

Clipped Wings

I am too old for your silly game,
Robbed of my childhood you used to proclaim.
But maybe if you saw it my way,
You would know how I value the things you say.

The beautiful words you so cleverly composed,
Over and over, new, or transposed.
Till you had me in the palm of your hand,
An innocent bird caught in quicksand.

I sink deeper and deeper till I feel a pull,
A feather was plucked, another, then a handful.
I try to fly but while I was mesmerized,
You clipped my wings, I noticed not your disguise.

You were a sheep in wolf's attire,
And resorting to a childlike mind, I was fooled by a liar.
This has never happened before
Because my precious wings I so adore.

I finally let my inner child free
Because of how greatly your words affected me.
But now I am stuck here sinking lower,
My flapping and struggling I must slower,

Or I will be swallowed whole by the sand.
As I keep my head up, I see you flee for land.
Abandoning me, childlike and broken,
This is the hooded cage I never wanted to open.

You Can't Have Your Cake and Eat it Too

Sugar and flour and butter combined
To become perfect and round and confined

Our hands did a tango with the whisk and bowl
Stirring until the batter became whole
Then into the oven to rise and fall
A rhythmic pulse as the chemicals brawl

But you pulled it from the oven too soon
Convinced me it had risen like the tide at noon
You cut out a piece with no care at all
Underdone and crumbs begin to fall

You grimace because it's not perfect as yet
But you did not give it a fair chance to set
You tossed away the cake we made
And all that was left was washed off the blade

You find a new recipe you want to make
But I stare at the mess and my heart starts to ache
My hands shake and my knees give way
I fall to the ground like the rain in May

I cracked the mold and your eyes turn away
No longer the perfect shape so you begin to stray
A rap at the door leads your hand to the knob
And in strolls the blond-haired blue-eyed heartthrob

As she grabs the sugar you whisper to me
Watch us bake the perfect recipe

Silent Static

Silence is loud.

Like the roars of an overexcited crowd

Like wind between buildings whipping

Silence breaks through the sound barrier, ripping.

There is no quiet.

There are pixels of an old television having a riot

There is the faint drip dripping of water from the pipe

Quiet enough but still not the *still* type.

Maybe true silence is real.

Maybe my brain protects me from embracing the feel

Of finally quieting the voices in my ears

Because silence is a member of my deep dark fears.

Sun

You had the sun and the blue skies
You had the clouds and its cold cries
You had the light that covered the earth
After the moon fell and the day gave birth

You would sit outside and enjoy the heat
A staring contest where you and the sun would compete
But then you started to carry an umbrella
Drama with the sky like a telenovela

Since when did the sun become your foe?
Since when did you walk and hang your head low?
As if concealing something from the omniscient sun
As if a terrible deed had already been done

The bright sun would gleam and watch you all day
For twelve hours until she had to go away
Then you would belong to the eyes of the moon
And the sun's heart sang a sorrowful tune

To Fester

Moon

That was the moment when it hit her full force
And for twelve hours the blood through her veins would course
It was finally time to see you again
So she sifted and searched through waves of men

Nowhere to be found enjoying the sun
Locked in your room where the darkness won
No light could reach you through the curtain
And all she feared was now for certain

She confronted the moon in the solar eclipse
And fire spewed from her furious lips
But the moon was unphased by the sun's cries
Because now she had the winning prize

The moon robbed the sun of all things good
A bandit of night like that of Robin Hood
For days the sun wept and flooded the earth
For all you wanted now was the sun to fall and the night to give birth

Tossing and Turning

I do nothing but toss turn and reminisce
On what was or what could have been–
Unless of course our kiss was just a kiss
A moment I miss as my hope grows thin.

Does he feel the way I do?
Can I trust this one will outlast the others?
Are the beautiful words he orchestrates true
Or am I a placeholder till you become another's?

A warm body for the cold winter night–
I turn over, the thought a painful jolt.
When I am with you I see lights bright
But they begin to dim as my instinct turns to bolt.

I force myself to rebuild my walls,
You did nothing wrong but I fear the end is near.
I begin to detach as my heavy heart falls.
Only my pillow remains to absorb my fallen tear.

Plain Jane

Blood boils at the thought of you,
Opposites in every shade and hue.
Exotic or another Plain Jane;
Take your pick, wrack your brain.

Plain Jane, chosen once more.
I am weak, tired, arms sore.
From clenching fists, knuckle to bone,
Slowly fading punches never thrown.

Tell me, tell me what to do,
Bleach my hair, make me new?
Exotic is clearly never enough,
But there is so much light you snuff.

So much more than just my looks,
My heart, my detailed life books.
Stories to tell, and new ones to write,
Jane's wind lifts you away like a kite.

Love was spilling and overflowing,
An unlimited resource, now slowing.
Rationed until my tree is barren,
Dry soil, my roots don't dare tear in.

The Night I Knew

The night I knew
It was over and done
There was no more sun
The moonlight grew

I sat on my floor
I cussed and swore

The night I knew
You were finally gone
I felt like a mere pawn
Was I nothing to you?

The earthquake hit
I indeed threw a fit

The night I knew
That you moved on
I choked down a yawn
The idea of sleep I threw

You left me in the dust
My heart nearly bust

The night I knew
You cared for me none
I became undone
As the white flag I drew

I lost a bet
With myself I fret

No Reply

I tap my pocket computer with weak might
Through my dark room a piercing light
No reply

I painfully wait like one who watches paint drying
Lying in a vacuum that is time defying
But no reply

The false concept that is time continues to pass
As I slowly feel my heart morph into glass
But no reply

With the hands moving on an imaginary clock
My glass heart cracks with each tick-tock
But no reply

A knock on the door causes the wall to quake
In death I lie from heart-break
No reply

Shards of Red

I told you my hurt and the state of my heart
And you knew that you held in your hands shattered parts

An aorta and two ventricles intertwined with
Shards of red

You gladly took my hurt and my heart
And stomped it into the ground

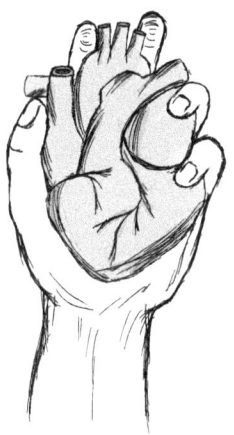

Home is Where the Heart is

You gave me your heart and called it home
A name I despised like the taste of honeycomb.
Sweet and sappy you tried to be
But you gave too much too easily.

I refused to comply to your heart's address
Afraid to confront your under-the-rug mess.
You unlock the door and let me inside,
Clean and pristine, what is it you hide?

Not quite visible to the naked eye.
But everything inside me said to run, untie
The grip you thought you had on me
I know it's an illusion and yet I can't flee.

You made it safe, too safe indeed,
I put down my purse like a farmer with a seed.
So deep I fell in deficient dirt
But how comfy your bed of lies and your oversized t-shirt.

I lived there a while, this home of course,
Like the blood and veins that travel with force.
But somewhere inside you became my lifeline
A drug I needed like an alcoholic needs wine.

Now you have me exactly where you want me
I am the captive you will not let free.
A controlled environment like a scientific test
I am the rat in search of cheese to digest.

You gave more than I was willing to give
You made me feel guilty till I begged you to forgive.
And then you started to pull away
Clogging the artery that kept us in play.

The house caught fire, like the ladybugs dreaded.
Where, my oxygen, have you headed?
But the arsonist took flight as he planned all along
Leaving me in a house I didn't want, nor did I belong.

Polished Porcelain

I stare in the glass at my own reflection,
Sad eyes gaze back in my direction.
Like a porcelain doll I crack no smile,
My color is dull, eyes run like the Nile.

I cannot look away; I am drawn to the mirror.
I wipe away fallen tears hoping to see clearer.
I tilt my head and squint my eyes,
Cries of brokenness beneath a brown hue, no surprise.

I break away and lift my heavy head
But all is well with everyone instead.
I glance back to look at my face, still the same,
But no one sees beneath my polished porcelain frame.

Behind Closed Doors

Waves ripple in the shallow ocean,
Welling and swelling, causing commotion.
Carefully brewing a great storm,
It barrels forward like vicious bees in a swarm.
Crushing everything in sight, a treacherous waltz–
It halts.
Crashing against a glass pane, but with strength it lacks,
It cracks.
The storm retreats as the glass did not shatter,
The pane is weak, but a strong enough shard of matter.
Time goes by and the pane is eroded,
Battered and bruised yet stands though overloaded.
The wave returns a grim reaper, seeking to destroy;
It's ploy.
Rushing full speed toward the pane, without smashing breaks,
It quakes.
The storm retreats as the pane plays a poker face,
Knowing it is as fragile as a fine vase.
When the water is nowhere in sight, the glass
Begins to crumble as it will soon pass.
Destined to give way, and the final blow solidifying fate,
It'll disintegrate.

The Aftermath

Cleaning up the broken glass.
Dustpan, broom, scattered shards.
A princess forced to sweep and clean.
But Cinderella made it look beautiful.

Can it Get Any Worse?

Before
The worst feeling was you not knowing I existed
The worst feeling was when my eyes met yours for the first time
The worst feeling was thinking I could never be good enough
The worst feeling was instantly liking everything about you
The worst feeling was thinking that you and I could never be
During
The worst feeling was trying to hide my excitement when I saw you
The worst feeling was thinking this was too good to be true
The worst feeling was watching you make time for me
The worst feeling was thinking there may be someone else
The worst feeling was you confirming my own suspicion
Now
The worst feeling is that I knew all along
The worst feeling is that you wanted me just to leave me
The worst feeling is that I would have been fine without knowing you
The worst feeling is that I am no longer the same me
The worst feeling is wishing we remained strangers
No
The best feeling is–
The best feeling is–
The best feeling is–
The best feeling is–
 It cannot get any worse

As Fragile As a Flower

You pick fragile flowers
But when uprooted
They wilt.
Why did I have to be
The flower you picked?

Don't Let Go

I want someone who will
Hold me during the cold nights
But not wait till the cold nights
To hold me

Why

The question that reverberates in my mind,

Overthinking outcomes till the answer I find.

Yet I always come up short,

Too many channels for my mind to sort.

Issues a, b, c, avenue 1, 2, or 3,

I sit in silence, mind churning likes waves in the sea.

I admit I know the answer, I deny it through and through

I fade away in silence for the why I know is true.

Full Circle

You said you would meet me face to face
And tell me if you no longer wanted me
And without a single word being spoken
I knew

I bit my tongue till my mouth taste of metal
And sat back
Allowing you to slowly and painfully break it off
At your convenience

Before I returned
You set out a seat of pins and needles
And when the day arrived
You pulled out the chair welcoming me back

You played dumb
As if you knew not the nature of our meeting
But you were never too good
At hiding your body language

I had to read you like a book because that day was
The most silence I had ever felt with you
Funny because like you promised
We were finally face to face

Hopeless Romantic

I harbor no anger that I was not enough.
Your actions, your words, I called your bluff.
I knew then as I know now, you did not want me.
But I never let you see my instinct to flee.

I knew, you knew, I saw right through you,
But without my cue you picked up the glue
And fused together my wounds of doubt
Winning your first aid badge, you hopeful boy scout.

I kick myself now, oh how I knew,
But I shoved that down and followed through.
Half-hearted, then whole, I gave everything I had
I have clearly lost my mind, I have gone mad.

The tree that keeps on giving.
But roots dry I muster for one more try, how unforgiving
This life. As I now have no roots buried in the soil,
I will wither away because those I love I spoil.

A blessing and a curse to want to give love.
Desperate I glance to the cruel sun above.
How can you produce light infinitely so
Without diminishing your heat, your color, your bright glow?

Do you give until you have none left
Or reserve just enough to not become a victim of theft?
You keep your word to shine your light
Even reflecting through the moon at night.

If you kept your word, like that of the sun
I would lower my walls, un-cock my gun.
But my foot falls victim to my atrocious aim.
A bleeding hopeless romantic only I am to blame.

Regret

Regret
I want to take it all back
Erase every memory till it's gone black
An open void with no end in sight
I wish and I hope and I shut my eyes tight

Because out of nothing, nothing comes
So if nothing is left, no trace, no crumbs
Then I am safe once more
Tucked away in a locked drawer

Never to see the sun or stars
Isolating myself like the planet Mars
But red and hot I burn with fury
And plead innocent to your one-man jury

Although I won your unfair case
No soul will know the pain I face

To Soar

Regret

But I cannot erase the mark you made
A unique scar as if homemade

Sure out of nothing, nothing comes
As zero and zero amount to no sums
But as instant as the theoretical Bang
I am filled with hope and a prickling twang

Deep in my chest cavity a beam of light
Protected from the ominous void's might
Though a scar remains forever
I now know I would wish it away never

A part of me I can always remember
As if branded by love's hot, hot ember
A love I did not know I possessed
For myself and so I can put to rest
Regret

Float

I sat back and watched her break
Barely floating in her own lake
A man-made body of water
A sitting duck waiting for slaughter

I sat back and watched her break
She treaded water like her life was at stake
The huntsman came
A loaded gun and deadly aim

I sat back and watched her break
With each step the huntsman took the ground would shake
Until the earth finally had enough
Giving way with a huff and a puff

I sat back and watched her break
Longing for the huntsman's gun to awake
But he wailed as he fell through the ground
And she basked in the deafening sound

Crayons

A rough paper wrapped around my torso,
Banded in black edges rather tasteful though.
Royal Blue forever branded by the iron's hot glow.
My story, my fate, I do not know.

Sharp blades of the sharpener scrape my waxy skin,
Creating a precise tool, the point thin.
Back and forth, to and fro I am used,
Tainting a white sheet, my color abused.

The child's grip tightens around my rib,
The same force practiced when escaping it's crib.
Pressure applied, I feel myself break in two,
Short story, cursed fate, if only I knew.

Sharp blades of the sharpener scrape my waxy skin,
Creating *two* precise tools, the point thin.
Back and forth, to and fro I am used,
Tainting a white sheet, my color abused.

Though split in two my colors still stain
Like jam made of wild fruits pressed through a strain.
A broken crayon still writes, though with pain,
My story, my fate, less I know, more I gain.

Never Touching Ground

You picked me up in your car
And we drove for miles till we were so far
From the city lights
And boring city sights

Your foot pressed the gas
And faster and faster I watched trees pass
I looked at you with fear
As your hands continued to furiously steer

Maybe slow down I implore
Because you shook me to my core
Then smashing the breaks I went flying through the night sky
Leaving you behind and never knowing why

As I soar I touch beautiful stars
Shining brighter than those of ours
But its peaceful here
Even if the *here* is unclear

Defying Gravity

Newton said it best
What goes up must come down
Like a bird falling from a nest
Like a barefoot Cinderella tripping on her dress

Newton said it best
What goes up must come down
You picked me up and spun me round
And sent me flying through the air

Newton said it best
What goes up must come down
But what would Newton call it
If I never let my feet touch the ground?

Love Lives

You used to laugh at short lived love
But at least their love lived
Whereas ours
Was never born

Phoenix

I blossom into a beautiful shade of red,
And flourish as my wing-span catches wind.
At high speeds I fly, like a snow slope and a sled,
Above the clouds I find my peace.
Not a soul for miles, open sky, yet with a sharp pain
I begin to plummet as my life reaches its lease.
Like a meteor I crash, only ashes remain.
But not death, rather the brink of conception.
Born again, a cyclical cycle like that of rain.

In Retrospect I Knew

In retrospect I knew
That the rain would always come,
The flowers would die despite my green thumb.

In retrospect I knew
The spring would bring about new life,
But soon face the business end of the cold winter knife.

In retrospect I knew
We couldn't bear the cold,
I am merely skin and bone, despite warmth your hands would hold.

In retrospect I knew
The glacier would always melt,
And add to the sea of icy pain, what a cruel hand I was dealt.

In retrospect I knew,
The sun would choose again to rise,
But not long enough to keep at bay the dark moon's cries.

In retrospect I knew
We wouldn't see the light of day,
I fear the night you seem to love so of course you couldn't stay.

Mourning

I think the worst part of grief

Is denial

Because no matter how much of the pain you remember

A piece of you still wants them to stay

A Lonely Stroll

I wanted to run through the sand with you

And watch our footsteps dance

Like a waltz

But I look down to see

Only one foot after the other

Dancing along

Protecting My Peace

Leave me be
I beg and I plea.
You decided to make the trade
So you must be satisfied with the decision you made.

You believed the gamble fair
My heart for a simple and short-lived affair.
I have come to terms with your sloppy massacre
And for you there is no more beating in my cardiovascular.

I believe in forgiving not forgetting
But when you call out to me regretting
You receive a cold and distant reintroduction
As if I did not fall victim to your destruction.

You underestimate my memory
Even though it was something I flaunted every
Opportunity I had
To the point you think me mad.

Perhaps I am to blame for the reason
You think my recall is in dry season.
Because I will do just as you do
And act like I never knew you, of course only when it suits you.

But please read between my cryptic lines
As you always did best deciphering around the confines
Of my sophisticated speech.
See how I am filled with life again you blood-sucking leech.

Excuse my French I am merely trying to continue the scheme
But truthfully life is now more beautiful than I could ever dream.
So I thank you for finally deciding to leave
But I ask you to not disrupt the peace I now conceive.

A Simple Life

Sometimes
Life is simple
And I am learning that
That is okay

The Cup and the Pitcher

The cup's deepest desire
The fruitful pitcher would acquire.

The cup was greedy and wished with the limit of the sky
In hopes of running the pitcher dry.

The pitcher caught on to the cup's game
And went through with the only plan that to mind came.

The pitcher pushed the cup off the table
Staining the carpet and tainting the fable.

Speak My Mind

Speak my mind they say,
But I choose to keep the closet of your skeletons shut.
I'm too shy they say,
But silence is a cover for the inner workings of my mind.

An organism that never stops moving:
My mind, constantly chanting, clouds my cranium.
My brain, a system that deciphers,
Nit-picking the multiple consonants and vowels you spew.

Information is out and about,
Flippantly flying through the atmosphere then dissipating.
Too consumed with responding,
You forget to listen, and so do the extroverts; you're safe.

When I speak my mind,
Trust that I can list each of your skeletons by name.
A woman of few words,
I require minimal consonants and vowels to speak my mind.

Checkers and Chess

Red and black or black and white.
I choose the latter with the queen, rook, and knight.
You choose the former, only seeing what's in sight.
Something only as real as a pixie or a sprite.

The fairytale you tried to tell.
But I am two steps ahead like a hound on a smell,
Watching the strategy you believe to be swell.
You dazzle me with magic, but I refuse your spell.

As bishops glide and knights protect,
You move red and black, but wit you deflect.
A skill I have mastered, evident by pieces I collect.
But you play checkers and I play chess, so it is clear, I suspect.

Clear that we do not see eye to eye,
Clear that I know you without having to pry,
Clear that you are like the others so no tears I cry.
Check mate again, but this time I spare my heartfelt goodbye.

My Prideful Portrait:
A Spoken Word Piece

Sometimes it feels like the thoughts in my head are reeling
But I have become numb to this feeling
Because it is a battle I always seem to lose
No matter how hard I try to corrupt the news

The devastating news of knowing I was right all along
Even though I wanted so badly to be wrong
Even though I did everything right
I followed the rules and talked through every fight

If this was a test I would have passed with colors flying
Being picture perfect because I was trying
To be everything you wanted and more
But right in my face you slammed that door

Neigh you did not have the courage to do that yourself
You allowed my portrait to rot on your shelf
Next to the head of another and another
And my portrait watched yet another that you smother

The oil paint started to run with lakes of blue
From my eyes to the floor and when you saw my portrait you knew
I knew everything
I would have loved to witness the plan in your mind spring

But instead I had to watch it unfold
And play dumb till the truth you told
And even on the day that we met face to face
I knew my eyes revealed what transpired with the girl in my place

My mind revealed all the possible avenues
But I sat quietly listening and waiting for your cues
That never came
But I let you get away with it because I refuse to take the blame

You will not pin this one on me
It was your mess that you will clean till you dig yourself free
From the enormous hole that you needed to fill
Because I was just not good enough for you still

I beg of you to light my devastated portrait a flame
To not keep me a prisoner on your shelf to see the next dame
That you let waltz into your sorry traps
But uh-oh you have buried yourself alive perhaps

Because when I walk in a room I hear you hold your breath
But if I recall you said my scent was "addicting like meth"
So if not my smell than it must be the thick soil
You're buried in because of that hole in your heart you need to spoil

Notice how my portrait is the only one with fallen tears?
Because you unlocked all of my unspoken fears
And maybe that was your plan all along
But let me explain where you read me wrong

On hands and knees I will not be crawling back
Because I have pride that you and your other portraits lack
Fool me once shame on you
But no shame on me because I let you reveal what I already knew

Outweighing the Pros

If a tree falls in lonely woods and hits the ground
Does sound still abound?

If I spend an eternity crying in my room alone
Then wipe my eyes and walk outside would anyone have known?

Yes to everything
The fallen giant and the puppet on string.

If there are no witnesses life will still occur
But only those privy to happenings outside of themself can concur.

So no wonder I knew before you cared to disclose
Although doors were closed you were never too good at weighing pros.

The cons always seemed to be more tempting
So I am glad I escaped from the false life you were presenting.

Sweet Denial

I am not absorbed by guilt
Despite how much of myself I gave.
I like to think
That you genuinely wanted someone
Who cares.
But
Who cares
That you genuinely wanted someone?
I like to think that
Despite how much of myself I gave
I am not absorbed by guilt.

Thank God

Now I sit back
Laugh
And thank God
That He pulled me out of the situation
I was not strong enough to stray from

The Here and Now

You will never know what it took for me to heal
How I had to drag myself from meal to meal.
How I cried out to God on my hands and knees
Begging for the pain in my chest to ease.

The sleepless nights I would endure
Because I suffered from an illness that had no cure
Since you as the doctor held the syringe
That I could not reach because of the squeaky hinge

Attached to the door that you slammed in my face
And the knob on my side had a deadly lace.
Two drugs you chose that can heal or cause a fatal blow
But I refuse to touch the handle that will drain my life slow.

I thought the wheel that squeaks gets the oil
But when I cried out in desperation you did nothing but recoil.
The hinge on my door tried to do the same
But you turned up your music to quiet what sealed the door to the frame.

So here I lie on the cold hard ground
With eyes shut and four walls around me that ricochet sound.
No peace or quiet as an ongoing movie plays in my mind
All our moments and memories tangle and rewind.

Now I can do nothing but feed answers to myself
And respond to the billions of questions on my mind's shelf.
The who what where when why how.
I restlessly problem solve till I arrive at the here and now.

Where I let joy and light seep back into my life
As your music and my soul are severed with a knife
Wielded by my hands that no longer tremble.
That are no longer fearful of how to reassemble

My life.
I am delivered from my suffering as if guided by a midwife
Until I open my eyes to see the colorful world
That with you was only black and white splattered smeared and swirled.

Looking back I struggle to understand my devastation
Because I am capable of an even greater destination.
Looking back I see that you pinned me to the ground
Prohibiting me and my potential to abound.

Happily Ever After

Although it did not end happily
I now bask in the happy ending

About the Author

Aly Mackenzie MacDonald is a South Florida Native. She is biracial, of Caribbean-American parentage. Aly grew up immersed in the arts. She began studying and performing dance at the age of four, and theatre from the age of sixteen. Now, a BA Theatre Performance Major at Florida State University, her passion for creativity is all-encompassing. She lives and breathes art in all its forms, and her goal is to dedicate the rest of her life to creating in as many mediums as possible.

This is her first publication as an author, yet she has been writing for as long as she can remember. Illustration was new to her, but she decided to jump right into the deep end after receiving encouragement to do so.

Aly hopes that others may not only find this collection inspirational, but also a source of encouragement. So, they too may one day soar.

If this poetry book has impacted you in any way, shape, or form, I would absolutely love to hear it. Please send any messages to Aly Mackenzie MacDonald at alymacpublishing@gmail.com

www.ingramcontent.com/pod-product-compliance
Lightning Source LLC
Chambersburg PA
CBHW050733010526
44107CB00010B/829